Sostenuto

Sheila E. Murphy

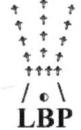
LBP

Luna Bisonte Prods
2023

Sostenuto

Copyright © 2023 Sheila E. Murphy

The author is grateful to the publishers of the following publications where sections of this work first appeared:

International Times, Stride Magazine,
The Argotist Poetry Online, Tinge Magazine,
Compass Rose, Word for Word,
Marsh Hawk Press Review, Blurb

Cover image by C. Mehrl Bennett

ISBN: 9781938521898

Luna Bisonte Prods
137 Leland Ave.
Columbus OH 43214 USA

www.lulu.com/spotlight/lunabisonteprods

Table of Contents

Sonnet	1
He Tells Me, Look, Look Around You	2
Hastening, Fastening	3
Overt	4
Sostenuto	5
And Then	6
His Each Morning	7
An Emerging Photography	8
This Passel of Commas	9
The Picturesque Anticipated Future Tense	10
Nor Am I Qualified	11
As You Were	12
A Grand Parade of Flutophones	13
The Threat of Rain	14
Our Lady of Tabula Rasa	15
That We May Someday Find the Courage	16
Pupils	17
Pre(sent) Tense	18
Detachment	19
Monsoon	20
Yet	21
Pretty and Smart Desiring	22
Gossipers	23
Middle Ground	24
Repertoire	25
Centers	26
Prayer of Thanksgiving for Rights	27
Please Pass the Courage	28

Portrait	29
Sight Read	30
Decision Point	31
Blue Camisole	32
Happen Stance	33
Staircase in the North Wing	34
Where She Churched	35
Just Keep	36
Another Word for Marigold	37
Dulcet Mid-Morning	38
Original Din	39
Esperanto	40
Getting Away (Party)	41
Mansion	42
In Peace Apart	43
Sheltering	44
May She	45
Mimesis	46
Caste System	47
Frames	48
Colonize	49
All The Days	50
Mantra After Mantra	51
The Conversation Is Not Milk	52
Barbara	53
I Think That I Would Like a Piece of Chalk	54
Try Not to Storyboard the Winter	55
Practice Makes Parfait	56
Sixty-Four Luxurious Ounces of H2O Each Daylight	57

Sonnet

There is an acrobatic sea upon me
And delirium invokes distraction
Once again the flecks of odyssey
Bemoan this sack cloth life repeatedly
Stitched in squares about to be
Extinguished like a mothwing
On the shoulder of entitled dross
Unworthy of humanity and yet
Humanity renounces itself loudly
Amid pale paucity cobbling leftovers
Vaulted into the breach when nomenclature
Suddenly dissolves there is no room
For anything but the boat the sails the struts
Desire

He Tells Me Look, Look Around You

And how pray tell can he know
The intimate surroundings of this
Accidental pedestal I imagine you
Imagine maybe even he
Imagines amid the inculcation
Requiring pomp affording
Stretch marks meant to last
Beyond a feeble lifeline proclaimed
By one palm reader highly qualified
Who is well acquainted with other
Luminaries in the field who once
Aspired to what turned present tense
In the glaring headlights veering toward
Induction

Hastening, Fastening

The easterly amendment of Christchurch energy
Has flawed me for failing
To rise as part of the uprising
In the middle of the upturned world
Imagined marble hued or silver
Splashed and frayed with circumstantial
Eminence within reason every interplay
Left to mean just dross falls off the corridor
half planned to mean reverence
Spaced from the top of the egg
timer reversal meant for all the world
To be a floodlight beckoning
To merchants and flabbergasted
Customers

Overt

Be my comma my apostrophe my breath
Mark in the sudden sleep the gift
Of maturation when the song lifts
From decibels to mirror leaf shine
On the lemon tree you fed
So yellow leaves would green again
To make a habitat for gentle and aggressive
Birds not far from geckos sprinting
Up the wall enclosing sacred privacy
We look out on hearing melody
Open like amazement in the voice box
Asymmetrical and love rich
Body chemistry kissed and
Lingering

Sostenuto

You will learn to love

What makes you capable of love

When stillness of pond stones

Intones within you understanding

That embraces where birds bathe and the sonority

Of place untouched that needs no music

Just allows your noticing

That nothing fills the present tense

Slow breaths mark the moment

You once thought to hold

Before you learned infinity

Meant something else meant not this

One thing sostenuto but absolute

Emptiness

And Then

Full of emptiness the scars leave
White places on the skin as if
Perpetually young defenseless
Perhaps resonant with the unease
That vulnerability might show or
The situation possibly recur
There's no utility in story despite
Incessant repetition of the word
Narration is a reflex adding up
To reified routine that teases
Scrawny probability makes it
Legend to float the concept
Of probability as if to even out the
Fear

His Each Morning

He likes the agitation to come
From him he thinks up lateral moves
That move the lemmings (they're all
Lemmings) in and out of danger
Nonsense and various he voyages
Through villages and major megalopolises
Splintering a previously orderly seen
Locus into willed chaos what does his each
Morning seem what does it bring except
Repeated playground images in which
His lack of popularity would show
So brazenly he needed to smother
That first truth with all kinds of new
Noise

An Emerging Photography

Now this everything at once becomes
Or is already true the high pitched
Interrogative *ah ummm* of youth to break up
Thought the sentence sequeling
Its way into advancement now what
To do with this how locate
A small umbrella to cover if not house
A batch of unlike things with
Zilch in common but this overhang
In shine and rain to mainline
Vigor back into the personality of
An emerging photography
That comes to look like me in
Fruition

This Passel of Commas

Shrapnel Nelle look out below
Above beyond the dimpling
Landscape clocking in with
Froth the myth of line drive palsy
Splayed now predicating vertigo
And teak and mad faced obliviata
Say you own all possible
Routes away you own
Consideration you own my history
My future breath and breadth
This passel of unwritten commas
Infinite and broad and deep
Her prior sleep the real
Infinity

The Picturesque Anticipated Future Tense

What is at the bottom
Where poisons various may lurk
I fear to touch in case
The map most varicose may clot
My voyage play hold sway over
The picturesque anticipated
Future tense replete with shadow
Mild or random placed
At some location firm enough
To spawn obedience that speaks to
Overcast or luminous sheaths
The mind draws in if not the soul
Mere body smooth drawn
Down

Nor Am I Qualified

Let me be clear: I have no right to tinker around
Things with which you are obsessed
And smirk, nor am I qualified
To purport to be above you
Your message and your choice of language
You are not billboard real nor virtual
How then can I just glance at and assign to some
Corner cubicle of my would-be art
Your life my form of entertainment
You are complete unto yourself just as I aspire
To own that same integrity versus
What I have been taught to borrow
From models celebrating their selfsame de facto
Ignorance

As You Were

Now I can return the church copy
Of *The Book of Common Prayer*
A member of the vestry told us
We could take and keep and use
Now I have a tiny white copy of my own
Direct from Cambridge that I can study
And absorb and treasure differently
In a quiet place and learn
What I rehearsed in that prior place
Where we were little known but needed
To be feeling among friends some of whom
Were friends and so shall be
As each passage reveals and lasts beyond
Longing

A Grand Parade of Flutophones

This window is about to open on
A grand parade of flutophones you can
Afford to keep clean with soap and water therefore
It is time to pipe up in unison if you can find it
And nudge a proclamation of majestic meaning
That we may leave to chance our snowshoes
And our Ugg boots and our sandals
Our Weejun loafers and our barefoot attitude and altitude
That we may stretch beyond the inklings and coordinates
Composed of latitude and longitude presumed to match
Some beatific foregone intent we fashion one step
Prior the next in the direction
Of a sacred moment transcending
Sacrifice

The Threat of Rain

What ultimately does the sunlight
Mean the same sunlight I stalked to quash
Ubiquitous Midwestern clouds that hovered
Near my head not soft voluptuous blankets
Of snow I am speaking of the darkness
Chiming autumn all the time
The threat of rain beside a feeble pinprick
Of light needing more of itself yesterday so what
Does near infinity of harsh hot sun
Bring to skin and the sad heart
Except perhaps the pretense anything
Can be forever as I believe your love given
Your track record of pure unrefracted
Light

Our Lady of Tabula Rasa

Our Lady of Tabula Rasa thinks me into existence
I begin now to encompass winter as a known commodity
That took me north by train to acquire
A little love with sheepish misunderstanding
Daunting in inappropriateness and known
Quietly learning to be at rest
Behind a window and fathoming informal unity
Made of the thought I work alone always
While being bequeathed a deeper and invisible love
Just palpable in retrospect where I reside amid
Ancestral lone saints who glisten
Like the foil of St. James in the capital city
Glimmering yet muted in precision consistently
Resplendent

That We May Someday Find the Courage

Ice rinks emanate sobriety in that caught way
Height hovers above the rest of us
While sheen reminds that horizontal motion
Bests the concept climbing as seditious thus
Demeaning of the whole of which we are a part
Invested in the grand totality replete with
System darkness that elaborates in peace
That we may someday find the courage
To bend down and honor gold that would transcend
The physical and indulge in genius grade humility
That walks the talk beyond incipient revelation
Sliding forward in chilled essence
About to be incessantly
Divined

Pupils

He homeschooled the children who gleaned adverbs
And disappeared he offered up his past for them
They sounded grateful as they offered madrigals
And safety and a failure to resist unusual ideas
He claimed were founded on ideals
The makeshift salience of oddments he proclaimed
Were sacred as the candles at high mass
He was vigilant about the blinds intended
To keep out neighborly interest he felt sure
Might be detained in some better universe
He claimed he would invent from scratch
By way of some new form of power better than
The sun devoid of chafing his metallic
Skin

Pre(sent) Tense

This morning I have recited moments of her life
That render her still glorious
Her perfect brain now stilled
Cannot change the constant curiosity
The striving the perpetual elegance
Her language still precise and picturesque
Revealing she seems strangely able to recall
With energy we share within
This tiny room from which
Her imagination launches
To other times and destinations
Glorious or commonplace she savors
As she tells me whom she saw and what each
Said

Detachment

You have stowed away the mother drunk
You have told yourself that people love your child
Born with a brain that does not think
The genius love at the center of your life
Starts to lose each morsel of that shining mind
All this your fault for not loving enough
While shade trees remain generous
You seek to learn the wind
Detachment turns to science and to creed
And you have none of it
You reach you grasp you hold you keep
There's nothing past the silence anymore
The three have gone or are soon leaving
Here

Monsoon

The heavy daytime darkness threatens rain
Thick summer holds just blankness
Thunder seems the precipice
Of soul smog decided not by me
Just dampening imagined joy
Of endless sunlight in which
I break even as insistent warmth to
Match my heart desiring more of
Early dreams those early days I prayed
Some source of joy I sensed
Existed somewhere mirroring a frost
About to warm to blossoms
Close to sky revealing the most accurate
Amulet

Yet

It's morning yet the day does not drone on
I have not meditated shades are still
Tipped down to block the daylight
I will absorb as I can cloister center self
Post-sleep my distant darling letter me
With syllables and loose-leaf proof
You love me mirror ways as I defend
My right to move in viable directions
As sun glints reassurance that this day
May sacramentally bequeath a gentle path
To sight read all my daylight definitions
Sudden soon and patched together from surprises
I would not intend but take as gifts or givens then
Respond

Pretty and Smart Desiring

She decides at lightspeed various vast
Things planted in the calendar that she obeys
Then claims to have completed
Each chosen direction and maybe exhales
Before she tells the story
That spells equally sudden regret
Before more fantasized freedom of motion
She'd like to claim appears
Along her windscreen she voices
Yet more desire and seeks agreement
To hold it as she hovers over
Territory almost claimed she hopes to realize
As soon as things work
Out

Gossipers

They lust to know things tiny things
They pose questions they weigh in on
Smallest unrelated moments
Of other people's lives they tell all they know
Resulting in uneasy audiences who cannot wait
To leave they perceive their leaking lives
Drained by needy predatory
People seeking one supposes
Currency importance standing
Anything seeming tangible unearned property
They lay claim to and continue hurling
Ever awkwardly a series of harpoons
At unsuspecting people clinging to private
Lives

Middle Ground

I sandwich you between irrelevant obligations
I cherish you I want to dwell at center
Where you are despite my obsessive rendering
Of an accounting of my meeting expectations
According to the life I advertise
The tasks I do not care about
The tasks appearing to define me
That in shadow do define me
As the things people can know
Both real and distant from identity
I know and do not share for safety
From the threat of piercing I resist to go on
Luxuriating in our shared our secret
Bond

Repertoire

Be my magnet anymore allow me
To extract the drum set thundering
From your driveway amid branches
Seeming to rehearse their casualness
I replace reflexively to match the prequel
Of my dreams a litany of buoyancy
Where divans float in madness
Evoking quotes meant for starlet dowries
No one can imagine anymore like floaters in the eye
These circumspect remainders of desire
How does that work given history hysteria
As variations on the theme harrumph
From novels plaguing shelves and
Psyches

Centers

Oh to sweet me oh to fracture history
Nibbling at my healthy heart
Thresholding sanity and sanctity
I crave I wash my hands of
And redeem someone this close
Or far away as if I know dead center
Better from a distance and revoke
The scattered rights of what unites us
Evermore the line drive less than linear
We grab like safety bars
To hold us upright that we might
Unify with safety what contains us
And invent what joy from recollection if we veer
Close

Prayer of Thanksgiving for Rights

I am not sorry I don't love you never loved you
Despite your innocent desire confirming logic
You perceived in our connection I was miming
What I thought was how the early years
Were drawn my eyes drew elsewhere
And I could not feel desire I tried
I could not make myself endure
The empty feeling of not wanting to be near you
You must have told yourself something
I could not hear I did not listen
And I wished the books you gave me
Could be placed elsewhere I could not fathom
Being interested in what you liked I could not want
You

Please Pass the Courage

Do you equate do you equivocate

Possession with intent let's be specific

Do you incinerate surroundings

You claim by way of possessive adjectives

That refer to life forms

And other scenery lacking heartbeat

Do you imagine these as swarms

That exist to prove the greatness

You surmise about yourself

When you stand before the mirror

Do you listen to your mirror

Do you observe your mirror

Confiscate your lack of

Courage

Portrait

She hesitated with confidence
To select the word
To show the truth
In a simple scenario
Requiring merely recollection
She found the word
She joined the word
With other words relayed
With clarity with poise
And gentle personality
A simple story she spoke answers
Carefully as breath in her wise
And quiet way of being
Young

Sight Read

All the white weeds near the cornices
Amount to a blancmange
Of scenic infancy across from shapes
And sides and seeds
The thought of kindness withers
As we watch the icing tease
Contrast from severance
Until a melody comes true
We vocalize to school
The precipice of tactile peach print
Overtones along the straightedged
Path the eye takes in
Absorbing fact and tacit wide
Arrangements

Decision Point

She stays in character once
She has decided to leave
Off the dross discontinuity tremors
Temblors the blue week stiffness flexed
Resembling an interior she fashions
She constricts to stave off
Original materials sin distraction
Call off nouns and call in artifice
To match design her feebling interior
Self-made self to wit a solo
Bandwagon propped up against
The way she started according to
The fools the sages her family of
Origin

Blue Camisole

Weather notwithstanding she undressed in view of
Lattices protective of near history
Of her fictional heart she overtoned westerly
Endearments catalogued inputs according to her study
Of the integers the Rubicon more silhouettes
Than can be counted she immerses her
Hologram in drowned things moments from this
Endowment she has named to mean
She means to separate from foundations stilts
Including generosity brought home to her
The limits of indulgence and the seedlings
Sprinkled like blessings upon a newly joined
Couple of individuals instead of
Rice

Happen Stance

Why not white out warbling for the nonce
The jealous birds singing in thirds
The Greenwich Mean Time sentencing
Of music as defined why not
Barricade falsetto arks replete with
Thudding selfsame personalities disguised
Distraught and seeking a way out
Why not keep the cinders polished
Brand or bright or solace filled through night
The slack tones of approaching trucks
The blue of salt spray beside the rocks
And cordial interference by well meaning
Neighborly constraints why not just
Bleat

Staircase in the North Wing

She is breathing she is breezing forth
She warms the lodestone centering
Her fantasy the cast of characters
She summons she defines denies decries
Her owned moments lift toward repeated
Skies and shining seascapes no matter
How divine the fine line between
Seek and grasp she draws in equally
The willing and unwilling to stanch
As if blood seasonally flowed as if
Memes could accommodate the variations
She defies all mood all winter all
Off-center variations on a theme
Desire

Where She Churched

She gave funds she knelt she prayed was seen
Wearing what distinguished her she lavished
Perhaps affection she was someone
She was physically diminutive she was spirit tall
She owned her things invented more she sat still
In the smooth pew she deflected she sang to
Herself afflicted with a gentle privacy turned harsh
She lived her mind her divinity was spun
To silver of the young soprano consistently afar
She watched the shallow world evolve
Her nature distanced paltry things
She seemed indifferent for focus calmed her
Toward the blue derivation of a constant
Innocence

Just Keep

Just keep lying still discover morning sleep
Recover patchwork of erosion
That revolves the inner door spinning
Sacredness spawning light to center
The canary in fictitious mine
Who needs syllables when mind
Repeats its calling and contains
The utmost kiss of sleep again
Is there sufficient space between heartbeats
How do they glow how know
Least sum of some of squares
Are strained to match magnetic wit
And pulse to shepherd steep
Immersion

Another Word for Marigold

Now is blazes past the center of my life and now
I live as if there were no history and any center after
Must be crafted in a new dimension ribbon green
And blue light that I know and do not know
As I resist recalling who I was as you defined me
I drank your wise voice I learned myself
By heart I thought I was inventing
With your guidance now I hover above
The strange facsimile of self you brought me
To another home that I had chosen
Then took to heart another lane that led
Somewhere so magical continued breathing
In the scenery your silken skin your constant
Light

Dulcet Mid-Morning

Good gentle daylight my reed thin elegant
Kind center with sweet spine
How I love your manifest entreaty
To extend the lifeline and be present even partially
As winter fades and thoughts of blossom
Shift the tree tips as a change comes on
I envision how breath becomes our breath
Hypothetically lengthening the breadth
And depth of us the sunlight draws forth
Forthcoming rain politeness fills the air
I know we have been always something
Now we know our rapture equals crystalline
And constant present tense even against all
Evidence

Original Din

She stayed in character performed her role
From the vantage point of other roles
Whose occupants remained in character
Sparks nearly missed the skin
There were imaginary fireflies immune to nets
The locus brimmed with salty talk
That rarely veered many feet from
The mouths that issued them as if declarations
Were meant if only marginally true
The din of this replicated original din
Everybody wanted to be famous everybody
Privately told the self this was already true
A curiously altered limelight met constantly
Moved

Esperanto

I keep imagining the parts fit together
Even when they don't I keep hoping
We are not a mere pile of puzzle pieces
With no emergent visual destination
I keep insisting to myself there's wholeness
Even as the edges fray so many hammocks
Where selves lie are pronounced semi alert
I keep arranging in my head my heart as if
The moldering connective tissue that joined us
Is not imaginary I keep remembering
A better future as I drew it in fine lines
I avert a long shot with short cuts I hear
Esperanto chimed by one big choir of
Us

Getting Away (Party)

No matter no spirit no wheel no world
What stopped being joyful spawned
Pursuits barely tethered to life choices
That slipped and fell and had to be
Revived the rambunctious soul noise
Spattered across windscreens
Of intelligible reverberations costly
Cheap in the vernacular there was no settling in
There was no relief of sunlight following
Brutal storms there were no fireflies
No stochastic mumbles no relief the pale
Wagering set sail and prompted paterfamilias
Fatigued with prior gardens still reeking with
Blooms

Mansion

Her nest is full of her
Acquisitions the hue of butterfly
The cry of listless parsed imperatives
As neighborly as any mansion
Close to topping in recent memory
Protected on a screenshot of the infant
Tide besmirched au naturel
Aside from habitual modernity
Over the transom in a minute pride
In prox to perimeters as oval as wash
Left hanging on the line in tandem
With the louvered doors hovering
And bandaged as if future tense were
Small

In Peace Apart

He tests positive there will be no more
Miracles in hiding there will be respite
Clear and near to heartfelt primitive
Heat waves and getaways long planned
I temperate resplendence as widows do
In peace apart from Piccadilly splendor
Close in physical geography with bells on
A bounty of recursion makes the case for
Every shallow grave with matching lawn
With matching fire place the mellifluous
Rehearsals and grace batched up
Before a cozy fire and brim light posing
As comfort as contagious as a cappella
Song

Sheltering

Oh that bouquets of positive outcomes would be
Delivered like multiple births and self-
Replicate all winter the dotted line relationship
Of pulse and mind and upstart
Near infinity to mark the start of all new
Past participles to wit indulgence
Due the undeserving and seldom served
Impressionable overcast eyes of new blood
In beaks and jars and gallon jugs awaiting
Stores of body accusations in the fresh texture
News one sweeps up on arrival as if
Sheltering the sane face from its surroundings
All feel and no soak time
Encroaching

May She

I hear the voice of seminar her sense of humor
The latent spiral of the mind advancing other
Minds alert to quarry and their decibels
Endowed with pearl shine of the books and
Breed of escalation lofted to the tip most
Freeing sense of thought she showed apart
From our own being taught the latchkey innocence
No one can imagine the abrasive speed
Of seeding one and then another holding in
The taut-weave basket that encloses
Minutiae we leave to selves beyond containment
In dithers and loose play of circumspect
Pale threads of sight read
Stories

Mimesis

Dance with her conscious of the wit light
Accidental sacrifice mimesis nearby integers
Epitomizing harbor mind and shelving
In particular housing glass and strata of
Windowed society as if only sentimental
Strips of shale can be capsized after
Homestead narrow as a path
And street sure chance flowers
Glimmering wild on grass shared thirst
That unifies polyphony before approaching
Witness protection that asks for seeds
At random without hope of return on
Investment as a lariat chafes the concept
Skin

System

Primary bedroom versus master everybody
Coast the ladder's propped the host wide open
If not awake the seashore quakes
Anybody been to Little Rock of late
Who lies in state the nick of time
The nicotine is rife who cares longevity
Is lost at cost the cinders pop the stage is set
The blazing heat loses steam in transit
The cost of doing business spikes the slide is set
To winnow till the slump subsides how many
Manacles does it take to fake the breathe in
Breathe out the better part of valor
The better part of mostly used up
Afternoon

Frames

Nefarious and various chanterelles give glow
To perfumed reserve slots chapter and versing
Singsong plenary indulgence free forming
Frames left out in the woodland of sleek bird lines
Cushioning the power flow in darkness and in light
To sway defray delay the housing countenance
She takes a shower he takes his time
The elephant removes the room from the equation
The blasphemed rope trick or penury
Leans down across the acreage the fog the wheat
Staging a comeback amid the shadow hours
Primed to weather what must come
Within reach the way we pilfer what we filter
Free

Colonize

Need a little extra practice need a venue
Need fresh reeds that can capture feedlot space
The territorial endorphins spores mistaken blasphemy
The tiger tailed elastic state of race
The cleavage of insomnia apart from parsing
The parsonage in full regalia prior to the mainstay
Happenstance and window dressing that shield
Undressing from frontal view or otherwise
The tacit momentum dried to lunge in spaced sextets
While peerage drones and sylphs its way
To jewelry and canards left home to their unnoticed
Caution moods a wild young otherwise
Night of chivalry elapsed in steerage where divans are
Stacked

All The Days

And I will dwell as leaves crush close to

Midnight's swan song

The imaginative sangfroid blur

Near shrill mind sharpness in dim wing light

Held in abeyance as I swift kick

Semi-opulence in the flat shins

Accustomed to the dance astride

An innocence acquired impending

As advance adornment

In division problems sorted blank

As white speed in the trill of

Intonation premising long tones close

To whole as cinders blink aloud and

Overboard

Mantra After Mantra

A creche needs warmth what warmth
Do you have to give what offering composes
Frets on the guitar what motion lies in
Wait in state do you possess replies intact
Do you imbibe in sacramental shame
Are there blithering unkempt receding hairline
Fractures in your present tense tell me
Slowly or swiftly your logic inmost poised
To deflate deliberations one-pronged nascent
Feathering the breaststroke inimitable
Within the makeshift dowry netting an indulgence
Cobbled together heretofore unplanned though scoped
Out of a tremulous blue
Wilderness

The Conversation Is Not Milk

We sight read mirror images and recognize
Old selves new selves patterns laced
With quiet that makes room for laughter
Once the softness cloaks experience
Brings us close again I hear what is beneath
Illusion I thought I sensed before now lifted
As the reverence of quiet time is laid across
What recollections shape smooth cloth we touch
And if a savoring can come as we begin our lives
From an accumulated learning leaves we know
Mean something drifted once now holds
And keeps us safe with faces
Just a little tired and calmer still
Warm

Barbara

First bossy friend made an impression I was comfortable
Being told to do something due I presume
To my capacity for hearing and not
Folding going my own way amid voice
Functioning a little light music in the background
She may have been unwanted in her home
She left and made her own and lived
A while in disappointment rumor had it
She turned happy toward the early end
She found someone perhaps resembling her own spirit
And I never knew her then but piece
Together now the little fragments
Of the flecks in hope that there were perfect lasting
Moments

I Think That I Would Like a Piece of Chalk

I think that I would like a piece of chalk
Please pass the chalk there are manifestos
To be charmed across the pavement sidewalk
Seen from flatbed seen from spa shark garish
Shine what wheezes past with lightning verbs
I think that I would like to document before rain
Comes and rinses off the Zen blink of this
Happenstance the cold the sear the elevation
Of the space between heartbeats I clock each night
I think that I would like to split in half this piece
Of chalk invite you to reframe what may be living in
Shared minds of people repetitively alive as one
And blend a little rigor with the wavy cloth of
Breath

Try Not to Storyboard the Winter

Simply live the snow and simply speak
The snow alert the selves within you snow
Is here to cool the selves within you
Simply speak the snow allow impressions
Of the snow to be the snow to blend
With what surrounds the snow including
Memory its own informal snow pretend
The water is the same as snow a relative
Found skimming across the cold sleek
Coating across land that just a little while
Ago was anything but white it was plump
Green then cracking leaves then dried brown
Limbs apart from all the gray conforming
Snow

Practice Makes Parfait

Nudge the crème de la deemed seedlings
Menàged with sugar eggs and spritzed let's say
With dappling sorghum missing making flavor
I promise I'm afraid of you I need someone
To bring the Buddha to collocate with me
That I may slough off yearning
For things for everything simultaneously
To last forever and immediately disappear
I numb my way to ecstasy I forget myself
For turning east just numb realizing
Anything any day now any moment can rise
Will solo stride and slide its way into the nebula
Less beautiful than your eyes still more
Predictable

Sixty-Four Luxurious Ounces of H20 Each Daylight

Prescribe me sunlight to afford unnested limb time

Just the anecdote to serve as antidote to crazy

Seeking to seep into blood veins well fed

Resistant to former friendly neighborly hypnosis

Turned pitted clotted wayward give me symphony

In G major to frame limelight maturely

As rigor pieced as multi-level love fest

Alive and well in fiction made to treat the spirit

To delectable possibilities more vivid than selfsame

Digs made from homespun scratch humility

Within humidity immune to fall guy penalty boxes

Boxed by hands unaccustomed to beauty apart

From wit-free power lust streaming illogic by way of

Marketing

Other Books
by Sheila E. Murphy
Published by Luna Bisonte Prods

Golden Milk (2020)

Underscore, with K.S. Ernst (2018)

YES IT IS, with John M. Bennett (2014)

Permutoria, with K.S. Ernst (2008)

*These books and
books by other authors
published by Luna Bisonte Prods
are accessible at:*

www.lulu.com/spotlight/lunabisonteprods

www.ingramcontent.com/pod-product-compliance
Lightning Source LLC
Chambersburg PA
CBHW060219050426
42446CB00013B/3114